THE
ILLUSION
OF
CONTROL

LEARNING OUR
TRUE POWER

WRITTEN BY

MIKE JENSEN

Live Life**Happy** Publishing

Published and Distributed in Canada by Live Life Happy Publishing.
www.livelifehappypublishing.com

Library of Congress Cataloging-in-Publication Data

Mike Jensen

The Illusion of Control

Self-Help > Personal Transformation > Psychology > Interpersonal Relations > Health, Fitness & Dieting > Mental Health

ISBN: 978-1-998724-21-5 E-Book

ISBN: 978-1-998724-20-8 Paperback Book

Cover Design: Mike Jensen

Live Life Happy Publishing

PUBLISHER'S NOTE & AUTHOR DISCLAIMER

To my incredible sons—Mickey, Blake, and Ryan.

This book is dedicated to you because of the profound lessons you have taught me. For so much of my life, I have sought to "control" everything—my circumstances, my relationships, and even the lives of those I love most, including you. But in trying to control, I only succeeded in creating struggle and misunderstanding, both for myself and for those around me.

Raising you three became my greatest teacher. Through the journey of fatherhood, I came to understand that control is an illusion and that the real power lies in influence. It took me years to realize this, but once I did, I committed to becoming the man and father I should have been from the start—a guide, a role model, and a source of encouragement.

Now, I strive to use my influence to support and guide you, to help you avoid the missteps I made. Yet I know your lives are your own to experience, with lessons to learn, challenges to face, and victories to celebrate.

This book represents my journey to freedom and true empowerment—a path I hope inspires not just you but everyone who reads it. My greatest wish is for you to find your own version of freedom and power, creating lives filled with purpose, joy, and authenticity.

With all my love,

Dad

TABLE OF CONTENT

INTRODUCTION

The Illusion of Control

Control is one of the most pervasive concepts in human life. From the moment we are taught to plan, manage, and organize, we are implicitly told that control is essential for success and happiness. Yet, what if this belief in control is nothing more than a comforting illusion? What if the very idea of control has trapped us in a cycle of unnecessary stress, frustration, and disappointment?

At its core, control is an attempt to impose order on an inherently chaotic and unpredictable world. We like to think we can control our thoughts, emotions, or even the behavior of others, but the reality is far less certain. The weather doesn't heed our wishes, and other people's actions are driven by their own motivations, not our expectations. Even within ourselves, thoughts and feelings arise spontaneously, often defying our best efforts to shape them.

The illusion of control offers a sense of stability, but it comes at a cost. By clinging to this false belief, we set ourselves up for inevitable disappointment when life veers off course. The harder we strive to control, the more friction we create—and the less peace we find.

This book is an invitation to shift your perspective. Rather than futilely chasing control, we will explore the liberating

alternative: influence. Influence is the power we wield naturally, through our actions, words, and presence. Unlike control,
influence acknowledges the interconnected, dynamic nature of
life. It focuses on how we can affect outcomes without clinging
to the illusion of control.

As we journey through the chapters ahead, we will disman-
tle the myth of control and embrace the empowering truth of
influence. By letting go of the need for control, you can find
freedom, resilience, and a renewed sense of purpose. Let's
begin by exploring why control, as we know it, is nothing more
than a mirage.

CHAPTER 1

THE FOUNDATION OF THE ILLUSION

"What if everything you've been taught about control is a lie? The harder you try to grasp it, the more it slips away, leaving frustration, exhaustion, and disconnection in its wake. But within that chaos lies a profound truth: freedom begins where control ends."

Control is not real. It is a concept we have fabricated, a narrative designed to make sense of an unpredictable world. From an early age, we are taught that control equals power—the ability to shape outcomes, to bend circumstances to our will. But this belief is deeply flawed.

The world operates on countless variables beyond our comprehension or influence. Weather patterns shift, economies rise and fall, and people act in ways we cannot anticipate. Yet, despite this reality, we cling to the notion of control as if it were a lifeboat in a stormy sea. Why? Because the illusion of control gives us comfort. It allows us to feel secure in an uncertain existence.

Control as a Coping Mechanism

The idea of control is rooted in our need to cope with fear and uncertainty. To admit we have no control is to confront the vast unknown—an uncomfortable and often terrifying prospect. So, we build rituals, make plans, and create systems, all in the name of maintaining an order that, at best, is tenuous.

Consider the planner who meticulously schedules every hour of their day. Each task checked off their list offers a fleeting sense of achievement. But what happens when an unexpected event—a traffic jam, a sudden illness—disrupts their plans?

Frustration, anxiety, and even despair can set in because the illusion of control has been shattered.

Control also functions as a psychological shield. It protects us from the fear of chaos and randomness. We tell ourselves that we can control our success, relationships, and even our health if we just try hard enough. This belief keeps us moving forward, but it also blinds us to the unpredictability of life. When events inevitably go off script, the illusion crumbles, and we are left feeling vulnerable and disoriented.

One powerful example of this comes from those who plan their lives meticulously to achieve a specific career or personal goal. Imagine someone who works tirelessly to secure a promotion at work. They believe that every late-night and carefully worded email will guarantee their success. Yet, when their efforts are overlooked due to a restructuring or an unforeseen hire, the illusion shatters. The emotional fallout—disappointment, frustration, or even anger—can be overwhelming because they've tied their sense of security to an outcome they never truly controlled.

The Emotional Price of Control

Chasing control often leads to emotional exhaustion. When we believe we can and should control everything, we place an immense burden on ourselves. We overextend, overanalyze, and overreact, constantly striving for an unattainable ideal.

This pursuit creates a cycle of anxiety and dissatisfaction. Imagine trying to control every detail of your career, relationships, or even your daily schedule. You spend your energy anticipating every possible outcome, crafting contingency plans, and reacting to every perceived threat to your plans. This level of hypervigilance can be mentally and emotionally draining.

Worse, when outcomes don't align with our efforts, we internalize the failure. We tell ourselves we didn't plan well enough, work hard enough, or want it badly enough. This self-recrimination perpetuates a cycle of stress and dissatisfaction, all rooted in the illusion of control.

Consider how this manifests in relationships. Many people believe they can "fix" others by controlling how they act, think, or feel. A spouse might think they can prevent conflict by controlling every aspect of their partner's behavior, from what they say to how they spend their free time. But this mindset often backfires, creating resentment and distance rather than connection. The harder we try to control others, the more we push them away, leading to emotional strain and disappointment.

Over time, the cost of this mindset becomes apparent. Relationships strain under the pressure of unrealistic expectations. Careers falter when plans are derailed by factors outside our influence. And most importantly, our inner peace is eroded by the relentless quest for something that doesn't exist.

The Truth Beyond Control

To break free from this cycle, we must first acknowledge a fundamental truth: control, as we perceive it, does not exist.

It is not a failure to admit this—it is liberation. Accepting that life is unpredictable allows us to shift our focus to what truly matters: our influence.

Influence is not about dominating or dictating outcomes. It is about understanding the interplay between our actions and the world around us. It is the power to adapt, to respond thoughtfully, and to create ripples of change without the need to micromanage every detail.

For example, in a professional setting, you cannot control the decisions of your colleagues or the trajectory of the market. However, you can influence the outcome through your expertise, collaboration, and effort. In relationships, you cannot control another person's thoughts or feelings, but you can influence the connection by being present, compassionate, and authentic.

Consider a gardener planting seeds. The gardener cannot control the weather, the soil conditions, or whether pests will invade. However, they can influence the outcome by watering the plants, adding fertilizer, and tending to weeds. Their effort creates the best possible conditions for growth, even though the result is never guaranteed.

As we move forward, we will explore the many facets of influence and how embracing it can transform our relationship with ourselves, others, and the world. Letting go of control is not surrender but a step toward freedom and authenticity. By releasing the need to control, we gain the flexibility to adapt to life's uncertainties and the clarity to focus on what truly matters.

Thinking & Review Questions:

1. Can you identify an area of your life where the illusion of control has caused stress or frustration?

2. How do you cope when unexpected events disrupt your plans? What does this reveal about your control beliefs?

3. In what ways might letting go of control improve your emotional well-being?

4. How does shifting focus from control to influence change your perspective on challenges?

CHAPTER 2

THE PSYCHOLOGICAL NEED FOR CONTROL

"Control is the paper shield we hold against life's chaos—comforting, yet fragile. But what if true strength lies not in control, but in influence?"

C ontrol, or at least the belief in it, serves a significant purpose in human life. It's not just a random idea we cling to but a deeply ingrained psychological need. Understanding why we need control helps us unravel the illusion and transition toward a more empowering perspective—influence.

Control as a Source of Comfort

Life is unpredictable. From minor inconveniences to life-altering events, uncertainty is woven into our everyday existence. The belief in control arises as a defense mechanism against this uncertainty. It provides a sense of stability, even if that stability is a fiction we create.

For example, think about someone planning a trip. They research flights, book accommodations, and create a detailed itinerary. This process gives them a sense of control over the outcome. But unforeseen events like a delayed flight or bad weather can disrupt even the most carefully laid plans. When these disruptions occur, the illusion of control breaks down, often leading to frustration or anxiety.

By believing we have control, we temporarily reduce our fear of the unknown. It's as if we're holding a shield against chaos, even though the shield is made of paper. This illusion may feel comforting, but it's fragile and unsustainable.

The Emotional Cost of Control

Chasing control comes with a significant emotional price. When we expect life to conform to our plans, we set ourselves up for disappointment. Every unexpected twist becomes a source of frustration, every unmet expectation a blow to our confidence.

Consider how often people say things like, "If only I had planned better," or "I should have seen that coming." These thoughts are rooted in the belief that more effort or foresight could have prevented an undesired outcome. This mindset leads to self-blame and unnecessary guilt.

Moreover, the constant pursuit of control is exhausting. It requires mental and emotional energy to try to anticipate every variable and plan for every possibility. Over time, this can lead to burnout, anxiety, and even a sense of helplessness when things inevitably don't go as planned.

Why We Cling to Control

The need for control stems from several psychological factors:

1. **Fear of the Unknown:** Uncertainty triggers anxiety. Believing in control helps us feel prepared and reduces the fear of what might happen.

2. **Desire for Stability:** Humans crave order. Control gives the illusion that we can impose structure on a chaotic world.

3. **Self-Esteem:** Success is often attributed to personal effort and control. This connection reinforces the belief that control equals competence.

4. **Social Conditioning:** From a young age, we're taught that being "in control" is a sign of strength and responsibility.

These factors create a powerful attachment to the idea of control, making it difficult to let go of this illusion.

A Shift Toward Influence

While control is an illusion, influence is real. Influence doesn't promise certainty, but it acknowledges our ability to affect outcomes in meaningful ways. For example, you can't control how someone feels, but you can influence their mood through kindness, empathy, or a thoughtful gesture.

This shift from control to influence is liberating. It removes the pressure to manage every detail and focuses on what you can genuinely impact. Instead of striving for perfection, you focus on effort and connection.

Imagine a teacher trying to help a struggling student. The teacher can't control whether the student succeeds. Factors like the student's home environment or personal motivation are outside the teacher's influence. However, the teacher can provide support, encouragement, and resources that create a positive impact. This approach is the essence of influence—doing your best within your sphere of power and letting go of the rest.

Letting Go Without Giving Up

Letting go of control doesn't mean giving up on your goals or becoming passive. It means focusing your energy where it matters most. Accepting that some things are beyond your influence frees yourself from unnecessary stress and frustration.

For example, in a job interview, you can't control the interviewer's decision. But you can prepare thoroughly, present yourself confidently, and leave a good impression. Once you've done your part, the outcome is out of your hands. Accepting this truth allows you to move forward with peace of mind, regardless of the result.

Letting go also means embracing flexibility. Life rarely goes exactly as planned, but adaptability allows you to navigate unexpected challenges with resilience. By focusing on influence instead of control, you build a mindset that is both practical and empowering.

Review Questions

1. Why do people often cling to the illusion of control? Can you think of a recent situation where you did this?

2. What are some emotional costs of chasing control? How have you experienced these in your life?

3. How does the concept of influence differ from control? Can you identify an area of your life where you could focus on influence instead?

4. What steps can you take to let go of control in a specific situation you are currently facing?

CHAPTER 3

THE MYTH OF PERCEIVED CONTROL

"Imagine waking up each day believing you're in control—your plans meticulously laid out, your routines seamless, your goals within reach. But then, a single unplanned event—a traffic jam, a sudden storm, a missed alarm—shatters the illusion. Control, it turns out, is not the steady ground you thought it was, but a mirage masking life's unpredictable currents."

From the moment we wake up, our lives often feel like a series of controlled steps. We plan, schedule, and structure our days with precision, believing we are masters of our own fate. This belief, while comforting, is a construct born from false assumptions and reinforced by societal norms. It creates a false sense of stability and predictability that masks reality's chaotic, unpredictable nature.

The Facade of Control

People often confuse repetition or routine with control. When we follow a set pattern—like commuting to work the same way every day or sticking to a strict morning ritual—we mistake consistency for mastery over our environment. But this consistency is dependent on countless external factors beyond our influence. The traffic conditions, the weather, or even an unexpected detour can disrupt our plans. These disruptions are stark reminders that our sense of control is a narrative we construct to feel secure.

Moreover, attributing outcomes to our own actions often ignores the larger web of influences surrounding those outcomes. For example, landing a dream job might feel like the result of your hard work and preparation, but the decision of the hiring manager, the job market conditions, or even a momentary impression—factors entirely outside your influence—often play pivotal roles. By failing to acknowledge these external forces, we reinforce the illusion that we control more than we do.

The Psychological Need for Control

Humans are wired to seek patterns and create explanations for the world around them. This tendency has evolutionary roots—our ancestors' survival depended on understanding cause and effect to predict dangers or opportunities. Over time, this survival mechanism morphed into a cognitive bias that overestimates our ability to influence outcomes.

Believing in control offers psychological comfort. It reduces anxiety by creating an illusion of order in a chaotic world. However, this false sense of security becomes problematic when reality inevitably diverges from our expectations. The more tightly we cling to control, the greater the emotional turmoil we experience when things don't go as planned. This turmoil is why embracing the concept of influence over control can lead to a more grounded and resilient mindset.

A World Without Control

Imagine living life free from the need to control every detail. Instead of obsessing over perfection, you focus on adaptability and presence. This shift doesn't mean abandoning your goals;

rather, it's about shifting your energy to what you can influence while letting go of unrealistic expectations.

For instance, a parent can't control their child's future. No matter how much effort they put into guiding and supporting their child, external factors like peers, environment, and the child's own choices play a significant role. Instead of trying to dictate the outcome, a parent can focus on fostering a nurturing environment and instilling values that positively influence their child's decisions.

This approach applies to all areas of life. Whether it's work, relationships, or personal goals, the key is understanding where your influence ends and accepting what lies beyond it. By doing so, you free yourself from the frustration of chasing control and open yourself to the possibilities that come with flexibility and acceptance.

The Role of Acceptance

Acceptance is not the same as giving up. It's about recognizing reality for what it is and responding to it with clarity and purpose. When you stop fighting against the uncontrollable, you create space for peace and creativity. This shift doesn't mean you stop trying; it means you stop trying to control.

For example, a business owner might face unexpected challenges like market downturns or supply chain disruptions. Instead of fixating on controlling these external factors, they can focus on adapting their strategies, finding innovative solutions, and maintaining a resilient mindset. This acquired shift in perspective can turn our obstacles into opportunities for growth.

Review Questions

1. What are some routines or patterns in your life that you mistake for control? How might external factors influence these?

2. Can you think of a recent situation where your sense of control was disrupted? How did you respond?

3. How does acceptance differ from giving up? How can acceptance empower you in areas where control is not possible?

4. What steps can you take to identify and focus on your sphere of influence in a current challenge?

CHAPTER 4

THE FRAGILITY OF CONTROL

"Control is a fragile illusion, constantly shattered by life's unpredictability. True freedom lies not in holding on, but in letting go and embracing what we can influence."

Control is not just an illusion; it is a fragile construct that often shatters under the weight of real-life events. Despite our best efforts, life's unpredictability always reveals the cracks in our belief that we can control outcomes. Whether through unexpected events, the actions of others, or the forces of nature, we are constantly reminded of our limited influence over the world.

External Forces: The Unseen Puppeteers

Think about the countless external forces that shape our lives. These forces, often invisible, exert a significant influence over what happens to us. For instance, consider the example of a farmer. They might diligently prepare the soil, plant seeds at the right time, and tend to their crops with care. Yet, the yield depends on factors like weather conditions, pests, and market fluctuations—all entirely outside their control. The farmer's efforts matter, but they exist within a larger system that operates independently of their desires.

Similarly, relationships are a prime example of how control fails us. People often believe they can shape how others feel or act through their words or actions. Yet, every individual operates based on their own thoughts, emotions, and motivations. For example, a partner's decision to stay or leave a

THE ILLUSION OF CONTROL

relationship is ultimately theirs alone. No amount of effort can guarantee the outcome. We create space for genuine connection and mutual respect by releasing the illusion of control.

The Domino Effect of Unpredictability

One of the most compelling ways to see the fragility of control is through the domino effect of life's unpredictability. A small, unforeseen event can set off a chain reaction, disrupting even the most carefully laid plans. For example, imagine missing your morning alarm. This seemingly minor incident could make you late for an important meeting, which might affect a work opportunity or a relationship dynamic. The more we try to anticipate and prepare for every possibility, the more we set ourselves up for frustration when the unexpected inevitably occurs.

Life's interconnected nature means that no single factor exists in isolation. Our actions are part of a web of interactions, each influencing and being influenced by countless others. Attempting to control this web is not only futile but also exhausting. Recognizing this interconnectedness helps us shift our energy toward what we can influence rather than what we cannot.

The Emotional Cost of Chasing Control

The pursuit of control often comes at a significant emotional cost. The harder we try to control our surroundings, the more resistance we encounter. This resistance leads to stress, anxiety, and often a sense of helplessness. The belief that we should be able to control everything—and the frustration that comes when we fail—can erode our peace of mind.

Take, for example, someone planning a wedding. The couple might meticulously arrange every detail, from the seating chart to the weather forecast. Yet, unforeseen hiccups—a delayed vendor, a sudden rainstorm—can disrupt their plans. The emotional toll of trying to manage every aspect of such a complex event can overshadow the joy of the occasion. By letting go of the need to control, they could instead focus on the meaningful moments and connections that make the day special.

Shifting Focus to Influence

Letting go of control doesn't mean abandoning effort or care. Instead, it means redirecting our energy toward influence. Influence is about understanding the areas where our actions can make a difference and working within those boundaries. For example, instead of trying to control every aspect of a project at work, you might focus on fostering collaboration and clear communication within your team. Doing so creates an environment where positive outcomes are more likely, even if the final result isn't entirely within your hands.

Influence also allows for flexibility. Unlike control, which is rigid and brittle, influence is adaptable and responsive. It acknowledges that while we can't dictate outcomes, we can shape the conditions that make certain outcomes more likely. This perspective not only reduces stress but also empowers us to act with purpose and intention.

Embracing Uncertainty

The idea of uncertainty can be daunting, but it is also liberating. When we accept that life is unpredictable, we free ourselves from the impossible task of trying to manage every variable. Instead, we can approach each situation with curiosity and openness, ready to adapt as needed.

Embracing uncertainty also encourages us to develop resilience. When we stop clinging to control, we become more capable of handling setbacks and surprises. For instance, a person who loses their job might initially feel disempowered. But by focusing on their influence—updating their resume, networking, and exploring new opportunities—they can turn the setback into a chance for growth and reinvention.

The Freedom in Letting Go

Ultimately, the fragility of control teaches us a profound lesson: freedom comes not from holding on but from letting go. When we release the illusion of control, we make room for peace, creativity, and authentic connection. We stop wasting energy on futile efforts and instead direct it toward meaningful action.

Letting go doesn't mean we stop caring or trying. It means we recognize the limits of our influence and choose to focus on what truly matters. This shift in perspective allows us to live more fully, with less friction and more flow.

Review Questions

1. Can you identify a recent situation where an external force disrupted your plans? How did you respond?

2. Think of a time when you tried to act like you were controlling someone else's behavior. What was the outcome? How might focusing on influence have changed the situation?

3. What are some areas in your life where you experience resistance when trying to maintain control? How can you shift your focus to influence instead?

4. How does embracing uncertainty open up new possibilities for growth and creativity in your life?

CHAPTER 5

THE POWER OF INFLUENCE IN ACTION

"Control may be an illusion, but influence is the quiet force that shapes our lives and the world around us. Like planting seeds, it's not about commanding outcomes but nurturing possibilities—and therein lies true power."

If control is an illusion, influence is the tool that empowers us to navigate life with purpose and resilience. Unlike control, influence is not about forcing outcomes but shaping possibilities. It recognizes life's interconnectedness and focuses on how our actions, choices, and attitudes can affect the world around us. By embracing influence, we move away from the rigidity of control and step into a more dynamic, flexible, and empowering way of living.

Understanding Influence

Influence is the ability to affect outcomes indirectly through our behavior, decisions, and presence. It is not about commanding or demanding, but about creating conditions that make certain outcomes more likely. Think of influence as planting seeds. You cannot force a seed to grow but can nurture it by providing sunlight, water, and good soil. Similarly, you cannot control how others will respond to your actions, but you can create an environment that encourages positive responses.

Take, for example, a teacher in a classroom. The teacher cannot control how each student will learn or behave, but they can influence the environment by setting clear expectations, fostering mutual respect, and providing engaging lessons. This influence creates a space where learning and growth are more likely to occur. The same principle applies to every area of life, from professional settings to personal relationships.

The Ripple Effect of Influence

One of the most powerful aspects of influence is its ripple effect. When we act with intention and authenticity, our influence can extend far beyond the immediate situation. Consider a small act of kindness, like helping a neighbor with their groceries. This simple action improves their day and might inspire them to help someone else, creating a chain reaction of positive interactions.

The ripple effect highlights the interconnectedness of life. Our actions, no matter how small, have the potential to impact others in ways we may never see. This interconnectedness is why influence is so powerful. It is not about controlling every detail but recognizing how our presence and actions contribute to a larger network of effects.

Influence in Relationships

Relationships are a prime area where influence plays a vital role. Trying to control another person often leads to resistance and conflict. However, focusing on influence allows for mutual respect and collaboration. For example, instead of trying to force a partner to adopt a healthier lifestyle, you could model healthy habits yourself and encourage them with positive reinforcement. By influencing through example and encouragement, you create an environment where change feels natural rather than imposed.

This principle applies to all types of relationships, whether with family, friends, or colleagues. Influence fosters connection because it respects the autonomy of others while recognizing the shared dynamics of the relationship. It shifts the focus from control, which can feel oppressive, to partnership and mutual growth.

Influence in Professional Life

In the workplace, influence is often more effective than control in achieving long-term success. A manager who micromanages their team may achieve short-term compliance, but this approach often stifles creativity and reduces morale. On the other hand, a manager who inspires their team through clear communication, trust, and support fosters a culture of collaboration and innovation.

Leadership is not about control; it is about influence. Great leaders understand that their role is to guide, support, and empower others, not to dictate every decision. By focusing on influence, leaders can build strong, motivated teams that are capable of achieving shared goals.

Letting Go of Outcomes

One of the challenges of embracing influence is learning to let go of specific outcomes. When we focus on control, we become attached to a particular result. This attachment creates frustration and disappointment when things don't go as planned. Influence, however, allows us to act with intention while accepting that the outcome may not be entirely within our hands.

For example, consider an artist creating a painting. They can choose the colors, the brushstrokes, and the overall composition, but the final effect is influenced by factors like the texture of the canvas or the way the paint dries. The artist's role is to engage fully in the creative process without clinging to a rigid vision of the final product. Similarly, in life, we can give our best effort while remaining open to the unexpected.

Cultivating Influence

Developing your ability to influence begins with self-awareness. Understanding your values, strengths, and limitations helps you act authentically and honestly. When your actions align with your true self, they carry more weight and resonance, making your influence more impactful.

Another key aspect of influence is empathy. By understanding the needs and perspectives of others, you can tailor your actions to create positive interactions. Empathy fosters trust and connection, which are essential for effective influence.

Finally, patience is vital. Influence often works slowly, building over time through consistent effort and genuine intention. Just as seeds take time to grow, the effects of your influence may not be immediately visible. Trusting in the process allows you to remain steady and committed.

Review Questions

1. Reflect on a time when your actions had a positive ripple effect on others. How did it make you feel?

2. How can you shift your focus from trying to control outcomes to influencing the conditions that lead to them?

3. Think of a relationship where you've tried to exert control. How might focusing on influence improve the dynamics of that relationship?

4. What steps can you take to cultivate empathy and self-awareness in your daily life to enhance your influence?

CHAPTER 6

THE FEEDBACK LOOP OF INFLUENCE

"Every action you take sends ripples into the world—ripples that return to you as feedback, shaping your next move. This dynamic cycle of influence holds the power to transform not only your actions but also your understanding of the world around you. Are you ready to master the art of the feedback loop?"

Influence is not a one-time action but a dynamic process that evolves over time. Every action we take creates a ripple effect, and those ripples interact with the world, creating feedback that can guide our future actions. This feedback loop of influence is powerful because it enables us to learn, adapt, and refine our approach. Unlike control, which seeks rigid outcomes, influence thrives on flexibility and continuous improvement.

What is the Feedback Loop of Influence?

The feedback loop of influence begins with your actions. Every choice you make sends out ripples into the world, affecting people, circumstances, and events. These ripples return to you in the form of feedback, responses, outcomes, or consequences. By paying attention to this feedback, you can adjust your behavior to amplify positive effects and minimize negative ones.

For example, imagine you're trying to improve communication with a coworker. You might start by actively listening during meetings and offering constructive feedback. Over time, you notice that your coworker responds more positively and starts sharing ideas more openly. This feedback reinforces your behavior, encouraging you to continue building a supportive communication style.

The Role of Self-Awareness in the Feedback Loop

Self-awareness is essential for navigating the feedback loop of influence effectively. Without it, you might miss important cues or misinterpret feedback, leading to ineffective actions. Self-awareness helps you recognize how your behavior impacts others and how their responses, in turn, affect you.

To develop self-awareness, take time to reflect on your interactions. Ask yourself questions like:

- How did my actions influence the situation?

- What feedback did I receive, and how did I interpret it?

- What could I do differently to create a more positive outcome?

Journaling or talking through situations with a trusted friend can also help you process and learn from feedback.

Adapting to Feedback: The Key to Growth

The feedback loop of influence is not static; it requires you to adapt continually. Adaptation means being open to change and willing to experiment with new approaches when your current strategies are not working. This flexibility allows you to navigate complex and unpredictable situations effectively.

For instance, consider a parent trying to connect with their teenage child. If direct conversations seem to push the child away, the parent might adapt by finding activities to do together, like cooking or playing a sport. By observing how their child responds, the parent can refine their approach, building trust and connection over time.

Influence and Collaboration

Collaboration is a powerful way to amplify your influence. When you work with others, you create a shared feedback loop where everyone's actions contribute to the collective outcome. This collaborative approach fosters mutual respect and enhances creativity, as different perspectives come together to solve problems or achieve goals.

A great example of this is a team project at work. Instead of one person trying to control every aspect, a collaborative leader encourages open communication, values diverse ideas, and ensures that everyone feels heard. The feedback from team members helps the leader refine their approach, resulting in a more cohesive and productive team dynamic.

Trusting the Process

One of the challenges of working within the feedback loop is the need for patience. Influence often works slowly, and the results of your actions may not be immediately apparent. Trusting the process means having faith that your efforts will bear fruit over time, even if progress feels incremental.

For example, an educator might feel discouraged if a struggling student doesn't show immediate improvement. However, by continuing to offer support, encouragement, and tailored instruction, the teacher may eventually see significant growth. Trusting the process allows us to stay committed, even when progress is not linear.

The Limits of Influence

While the feedback loop of influence is powerful, it's important to recognize its limits. Not every action will yield the desired result, and not every situation can be influenced. Understanding these boundaries helps you avoid unnecessary frustration and focus your energy where it can have the greatest impact.

For example, trying to change someone's deeply held beliefs might prove fruitless if they are unwilling to engage in dialogue. In such cases, your role might be to plant seeds of thought rather than expect immediate change. Recognizing the limits of your influence allows you to let go of unattainable goals and focus on areas where you can make a meaningful difference.

Review Questions

1. Reflect on a time when you received feedback after influencing a situation. How did you use that feedback to adjust your approach?

2. How can self-awareness help you navigate the feedback loop of influence more effectively?

3. Think of a recent collaboration. How did the feedback loop within the group shape the outcome? What role did you play in that process?

4. What steps can you take to trust the process of influence, even when progress feels slow or uncertain?

CHAPTER 7

EMBRACING THE UNKNOWN

*"Life's greatest possibilities lie in the unknown
—what if embracing uncertainty isn't something to
fear, but the key to unlocking your potential?"*

L ife is full of uncertainties. From the small unpredictabilities of daily life to the larger unknowns of our future, uncertainty is a constant companion. While it can be daunting, uncertainty is also what makes life dynamic and full of possibilities. Instead of fearing it, we can learn to navigate uncertainty with confidence and grace by focusing on influence rather than control. Taking on the unknown allows us to experience growth, discovery, and resilience.

Why Uncertainty Feels Uncomfortable

Humans are wired to seek patterns and predictability. It's an evolutionary survival mechanism that helped our ancestors anticipate danger and plan for the future. However, in modern life, this instinct often creates anxiety when faced with ambiguity. The idea of not knowing what comes next can make us feel vulnerable and unprepared.

For example, waiting for the outcome of a job interview can be nerve-wracking. The uncertainty of whether you'll get the job might lead to overthinking, second-guessing your performance, or imagining worst-case scenarios. This discomfort stems from our desire to control outcomes and avoid the unknown.

Shifting Perspective: Uncertainty as Opportunity

Instead of believing uncertainty is a threat, we can decide to see it as an opportunity. The unknown is where possibilities exist. It's the space where innovation, creativity, and growth thrive. When we let go of the need to predict or control, we free ourselves to explore new paths and embrace unexpected opportunities.

Take, for instance, someone moving to a new city. While the uncertainty of adapting to a new environment can be intimidating, it also offers the chance to meet new people, discover different cultures, and gain fresh perspectives. They can turn the experience into a positive and enriching journey by focusing on the possibilities rather than the risks.

The Role of Influence in Uncertainty

When faced with uncertainty, the key is to focus on what you can influence. Influence allows you to take purposeful actions without being attached to specific outcomes. For example, if you're preparing for a presentation, you can't control how the audience will react, but you can influence their experience by delivering a clear and engaging message.

This approach shifts your energy from worrying about what's beyond your control to actively shaping what's within your reach. It's not about eliminating uncertainty but about navigating it with confidence and intention.

Developing Resilience Through Uncertainty

Resilience is our ability to be flexible and bounce back from challenges. It's a vital skill for navigating uncertainty because it helps you stay grounded and focused, even when things don't go as planned. Developing resilience starts with accepting that uncertainty is a natural part of life.

One way to build resilience is by practicing mindfulness. Mindfulness helps you stay present and focused, reducing the tendency to dwell on fears about the future. You can approach uncertainty with a clear and calm mind by grounding yourself in the present moment.

Another way to strengthen resilience is by reframing setbacks as learning opportunities. Instead of seeing failure as an undesired ending, view it as a directional step to growth. For example, if a business adventure doesn't succeed, you can analyze what went wrong, learn from what went wrong, and apply those lessons to future decisions.

The Power of Adaptability

Adaptability is the ability to adjust to changing circumstances. It's a crucial skill for navigating uncertainty because it allows you to pivot and find new solutions when faced with unexpected challenges. Adaptability requires a willingness to release the concrete plans and embrace flexibility.

For instance, during the COVID-19 pandemic, many businesses had to adapt quickly to survive. Restaurants shifted to takeout and delivery services, while office workers transitioned to remote work. Those who embraced adaptability were better equipped to navigate the uncertainty and find creative ways to move forward.

Embracing the Present Moment

Uncertainty often pulls our attention to the future, filling our minds with "what if" scenarios. To counter this, practice embracing the present moment. The present is the only time where action and influence are possible. Focusing on what you can do right now reduces anxiety and creates a sense of empowerment.

For example, if you're worried about an upcoming exam, focus on studying and preparing in the present instead of fixating on the possible outcomes. By channeling your energy into productive actions, you'll feel more in control of your efforts and better equipped to handle the results, whatever they may be.

Letting Go of the Illusion of Control

Letting go of control doesn't mean giving up; it means recognizing the limits of your influence and focusing your energy where it matters most. This mindset shift frees you from the frustration of trying to manage the unmanageable and allows you to approach uncertainty with a sense of peace.

For instance, imagine planning an outdoor event. You can't control the weather, but you can prepare for different possibilities by arranging tents or alternative indoor venues. By focusing on what you can influence, you're able to enjoy the event without being overwhelmed by worry.

Review Questions

1. Reflect on a recent situation where you faced uncertainty. How did you respond, and what could you have done differently?

2. How can you reframe uncertainty as an opportunity rather than a threat?

3. How can practicing mindfulness help you navigate uncertain situations in your daily life?

4. Think of a time when adaptability helped you overcome a challenge. What did you learn from the experience?

CHAPTER 8

RELATIONSHIPS WITHOUT CONTROL

"We can't fix others, control their choices, or dictate their feelings—but we can influence them in ways that build trust, deepen connections, and foster growth. True power in relationships lies not in control, but in understanding, respect, and collaboration."

Human relationships are at the heart of our lives. From family and friendships to romantic and professional connections, relationships shape our experiences and influence our happiness. Yet, relationships are also one of the areas where people most often struggle with the illusion of control. Many believe they can "fix" others, dictate behaviors, or manage outcomes, but these attempts at control frequently lead to conflict and disappointment. To build stronger, more fulfilling relationships, we must shift from control to influence.

The Illusion of Control in Relationships

Control in relationships often stems from good intentions. A parent might try to control a child's choices to protect them. A partner might attempt to steer the relationship to avoid pain or conflict. While these efforts come from a place of care, they ignore the autonomy of the other person.

The reality is that we cannot control another person's thoughts, feelings, or actions. Each individual has their own experiences, motivations, and desires. Trying to impose control over someone else often leads to resistance, resentment, and tension. For example, a spouse trying to change their partner's habits through nagging or criticism may only push them further away.

Influence as a Foundation for Connection

Instead of control, influence provides a healthier and more effective way to foster meaningful relationships. Influence respects the other person's autonomy while focusing on building trust, understanding, and collaboration.

Consider a parent who wants their teenager to prioritize schoolwork. Rather than trying to force compliance through punishment or strict rules, the parent could influence by demonstrating the value of education, engaging in supportive conversations, and providing a structured environment. This approach encourages cooperation rather than rebellion.

Influence is also about leading by example. If you want someone to be more open and communicative, show vulnerability and honesty in your own interactions. By modeling the behavior you wish to see, you create an environment where others feel safe to reciprocate.

Building Trust Through Influence

Trust is the cornerstone of influence. Without trust, even well-meaning efforts to guide or support someone can be met with skepticism or resistance. To build trust, focus on these key principles:

1. **Consistency:** Follow through on your promises and show reliability. Consistent actions build a foundation of trust over time.

2. **Empathy:** Show genuine care and understanding for the other person's feelings and experiences. Listen actively and validate their emotions.

3. **Authenticity:** Be honest and true to your intentions. People are more likely to trust you when they sense that your actions align with your values.

Trust allows relationships to flourish. When someone trusts you, they are more likely to be open to your influence because they feel safe and respected.

Navigating Conflict Without Control

Conflict is a natural part of any relationship, but how we approach it can make a significant difference. Attempting to control the outcome of a conflict often escalates tensions. Instead, focus on influence by seeking common ground and fostering constructive dialogue.

For example, in a disagreement with a coworker, rather than insisting on your viewpoint, try to understand their perspective. Ask questions, acknowledge their concerns, and look for solutions that benefit both parties. By prioritizing collaboration over control, you create an atmosphere where conflict can be resolved productively.

The Freedom of Letting Go

Letting go of control in relationships doesn't mean becoming passive or indifferent. It means recognizing the limits of your influence and respecting the autonomy of others. This mindset shift allows you to focus on what truly matters: connection, communication, and mutual growth.

For instance, a friend struggling with a personal issue might not respond to your advice or support in the way you'd hoped. Instead of feeling frustrated or defeated, focus on being present and available. Sometimes, simply offering a listening ear or a comforting presence is the most powerful way to influence.

Letting go of control also frees you from unnecessary stress. When you release the need to manage every outcome, you create space for relationships to evolve naturally. This openness often leads to deeper and more authentic connections.

Practical Steps to Shift from Control to Influence

1. **Practice Active Listening:** Pay attention to what the other person is saying without interrupting or planning your response. This active listening shows respect and builds understanding.

2. **Focus on Your Actions:** Instead of trying to change someone else, reflect on how you can influence the situation through your behavior and attitude.

3. **Encourage Autonomy:** Support the other person's ability to make their own choices. Offer guidance when asked, but respect their decisions.

4. **Model the Behavior You Want to See:** Lead by example. Your actions often speak louder than words.

5. **Let Go of Outcomes:** Accept that you cannot control how others respond to your influence. Focus on doing your best and trust the process.

Review Questions

1. Reflect on a relationship where you've tried to exert control. How did it impact the connection, and what could you have done differently?

2. Think of a time when someone influenced you positively. What qualities did they demonstrate, and how did it affect your behavior?

3. How can building trust improve your ability to influence others in your relationships?

4. What steps can you take to let go of control and focus on fostering connection and collaboration?

CHAPTER 9

INFLUENCE AND LEADERSHIP

"Leadership isn't about controlling—it's about empowering others to grow and be successful too. True leaders inspire trust, collaboration, and innovation, proving that influence, not authority, is the foundation of lasting success."

Leadership is one of the clearest examples of how influence surpasses control in effectiveness. Whether in the workplace, community, or family, leaders who focus on influence foster growth, collaboration, and innovation. In contrast, those who rely on control often face resistance, disengagement, and limited results. True leadership recognizes the power of influence to inspire and empower others, creating an environment where individuals thrive and collective goals are achieved.

Leadership Without Control

Many people equate leadership with authority or control, but this view is outdated and ineffective. Leadership is not about giving orders or micromanaging tasks but guiding, supporting, and inspiring others. A leader who relies on control may achieve short-term compliance, but they stifle creativity, motivation, and trust in the long run.

Consider a manager who insists on approving every decision and monitoring every task. This approach may keep projects on track temporarily, but it also creates a culture of dependency and fear. Employees may feel hesitant to take initiative or offer new ideas, fearing they'll be overruled or criticized. In contrast, a leader who empowers their team to make decisions and contribute ideas fosters a sense of ownership and confidence, leading to better results.

The Role of Influence in Leadership

Influence is at the heart of effective leadership. It's about inspiring others to share your vision and work toward common goals. This approach requires clear communication, emotional intelligence, and the ability to build strong relationships. When leaders focus on influence, they create an environment where people feel valued, motivated, and capable of achieving great things.

For example, a teacher who encourages their students to think critically and explore their interests is influencing them to develop a love of learning. By supporting their growth and fostering curiosity, the teacher sets the stage for lifelong success.

Building Trust as a Leader

Trust is essential for leadership through influence. People are less likely to follow your guidance or embrace your vision without trust. To build trust, leaders must demonstrate consistency, empathy, and integrity:

1. **Consistency:** Follow through on your commitments and maintain a steady approach to decision-making. Consistency builds credibility and reliability.

2. **Empathy:** Show genuine care for the needs and concerns of your team. Listen actively and validate their experiences.

3. **Integrity:** Lead by example and act in alignment with your values. When people see that your actions match your words, they're more likely to trust and respect you.

Encouraging Collaboration

Collaboration is a powerful tool for leaders who prioritize influence. By fostering teamwork and valuing diverse perspectives, leaders can achieve results that far surpass what any individual could accomplish alone. Collaboration also strengthens relationships, builds trust, and encourages creative problem-solving.

For instance, a community leader organizing a neighborhood improvement project might invite input from residents about their priorities and ideas. By involving everyone in the process, the leader not only generates better solutions but also builds a sense of unity and shared purpose.

Empowering Others

Empowerment is one of the most impactful ways leaders can use influence. When leaders empower others, they trust them to take initiative, make decisions, and contribute their unique strengths. Empowerment fosters a sense of ownership and accountability, leading to greater engagement and better outcomes.

A business leader, for example, might empower their team by delegating important responsibilities and providing the resources and support needed for success. This approach not only builds confidence within the team but also enables the leader to focus on strategic priorities rather than getting bogged down in details.

Navigating Challenges as a Leader

Leadership is not without its challenges. There will be times when conflicts arise, goals are missed, or unexpected obstacles emerge. It's tempting to revert to control in these moments to regain a sense of order. However, effective leaders use challenges as opportunities to deepen their influence.

For example, during a project delay, a leader might convene their team to identify the root causes and brainstorm solutions. By involving the team in problem-solving, the leader not only addresses the immediate issue but also strengthens the team's ability to handle future challenges collaboratively.

Balancing Influence and Accountability

While influence is key to leadership, it must be balanced with accountability. Leaders are responsible for setting clear expectations, providing guidance, and ensuring progress toward goals. This balance requires clarity, communication, and a willingness to address issues constructively.

For example, a sports coach might influence their players by inspiring them to give their best effort, but they also hold the team accountable for showing up to practice and adhering to game plans. This balance creates an environment where people feel supported and motivated while understanding the importance of discipline and commitment.

Practical Steps for Leadership Through Influence

1. **Communicate Clearly:** Share your vision and goals in a way that inspires and motivates others. Be transparent and open to feedback.

2. **Build Relationships:** Invest time in understanding the needs, strengths, and concerns of those you lead. Strong relationships are the foundation of influence.

3. **Foster Collaboration:** Encourage teamwork and value diverse perspectives. Create opportunities for people to contribute and feel included.

4. **Empower Others:** Delegate responsibilities and trust people to take ownership of their work. Provide support and resources as needed.

5. **Model Resilience:** Show how to handle challenges with grace and adaptability. Your response to setbacks sets the energy for your team.

Review Questions

1. Reflect on a leader you admire. How did they use influence rather than control to guide and inspire others?

2. Think of a situation where you were in a leadership role. How did you balance influence and accountability?

3. What steps can you take to build trust and foster collaboration in your own leadership efforts?

4. How can empowering others enhance your effectiveness as a leader and strengthen your relationships?

CHAPTER 10

BREAKING FREE FROM LIMITING BELIEFS

"Beliefs can either be the wings that lift us or the chains that hold us back. What invisible barriers are shaping your life—and are you ready to break free?"

The beliefs we hold shape our experiences and guide our decisions. While some beliefs empower us, others create invisible barriers that limit our potential. These limiting beliefs often stem from the illusion of control, convincing us that we must manage every aspect of our lives to succeed. Breaking free from these mental constraints is essential for embracing influence and living authentically.

What Are Limiting Beliefs?

Limiting beliefs are assumptions or perceptions that we accept as true but which restrict our actions or potential. These beliefs often develop over time through experiences, cultural influences, or internalized messages from others. For example, someone might believe, "I'm not good at public speaking," or "I can't succeed unless everything goes perfectly." While these beliefs feel real, they are often based on fear rather than fact.

The illusion of control frequently fuels limiting beliefs. When we believe that success depends entirely on our ability to control outcomes, we may avoid risks, fear failure, or place unrealistic expectations on ourselves. Acknowledging these patterns is the first step to breaking free.

How Limiting Beliefs Develop

1. **Past Experiences:** Negative experiences can create limiting beliefs. For instance, failing a test as a child might lead to the belief, "I'm not smart enough."

2. **Cultural Influences:** Societal norms and expectations can instill beliefs about what is possible or acceptable. For example, cultural messages about gender roles can shape career aspirations.

3. **Fear of Uncertainty:** The need for control often arises from a fear of the unknown. This fear can manifest as beliefs that prioritize safety and predictability over growth and exploration.

Identifying Your Limiting Beliefs

To break free from limiting beliefs, you must first identify them. Here are some steps to uncover the beliefs that may be holding you back:

1. **Listen to Your Inner Dialogue:** Pay attention to the thoughts that arise when you face challenges or new opportunities. Phrases like "I can't" or "I'm not good at" often signal limiting beliefs.

2. **Examine Patterns:** Reflect on areas of your life where you feel stuck or dissatisfied. Are there recurring thoughts or behaviors that reinforce the status quo?

3. **Challenge Assumptions:** Question the validity of your beliefs. Ask yourself, "Is this really true?" or "What actual proof do I have to support this belief?"

Shifting Your Mindset

Once you've identified your limiting beliefs, the next step is to replace them with empowering alternatives. This shift requires intentional effort and practice, but can transform your perspective and open new possibilities.

1. **Reframe Negative Thoughts:** Turn limiting beliefs into positive affirmations. For example, replace "I can't handle change" with "I am adaptable and capable of navigating new situations."

2. **Focus on Growth:** Embrace a growth mindset by viewing challenges as opportunities to learn and improve. Instead of being afraid of failure, see it as the next step on a path to success.

3. **Celebrate Progress:** Acknowledge small wins and incremental growth. This awareness reinforces your ability to influence outcomes and builds confidence over time.

Letting Go of Perfectionism

Perfectionism is a common manifestation of the illusion of control. The belief that everything must be flawless often leads to procrastination, burnout, and dissatisfaction. Letting go of perfectionism allows you to focus on progress and embrace imperfection as part of the journey.

Consider a student who delays submitting an assignment because it isn't perfect. This fear of imperfection creates unnecessary stress and limits their ability to learn and grow. By accepting that imperfection is natural, they can take action and build confidence in their abilities.

Building Confidence Through Action

Confidence grows through action, not control. Taking small, consistent steps toward your goals reinforces your ability to influence outcomes. Each action, no matter how small, builds momentum and reduces the power of limiting beliefs.

For example, someone who fears public speaking might start by speaking in front of a trusted friend or joining a small group discussion. Over time, these small actions build confidence and dispel the belief that public speaking is insurmountable.

The Freedom of Releasing Limiting Beliefs

Letting go of limiting beliefs creates space for authenticity and empowerment. When you release the need to control everything, you allow yourself to explore new possibilities and embrace the uncertainty of growth. This freedom enables you to live more fully, with less fear and more joy.

Practical Steps to Overcome Limiting Beliefs

1. **Identify Triggers:** Recognize situations that activate your limiting beliefs and reflect on why they arise.

2. **Create Affirmations:** Write down positive ideas and quotes that counteract your limiting beliefs and repeat them daily.

3. **Seek Support:** Surround yourself with mentors and individuals who encourage and challenge you to grow. Their perspectives can help you see beyond your own mental constraints.

4. **Take Risks:** Step outside your comfort zone and try new things, even if they feel uncomfortable. Each step builds resilience and weakens the grip of limiting beliefs.

Review Questions

1. What limiting beliefs have held you back in the past, and how did they develop?

2. Reflect on a recent challenge. How did your beliefs influence your approach and outcome?

3. What steps can you take to replace a specific limiting belief with a more empowering alternative?

4. How can letting go of perfectionism help you focus on growth and progress?

CHAPTER 11

REDEFINING SUCCESS

"What if the success you're chasing isn't really your own? Imagine redefining success—not as what you achieve, but as how you grow, adapt, and influence the world around you. It's time to shift the narrative."

S uccess is often defined by external achievements: a high-paying job, a big house, or widespread recognition. These markers, while celebrated by society, are often tied to the illusion of control—the belief that we must meet specific standards to prove our worth. This narrow definition of success can leave us feeling stressed, inadequate, or unfulfilled. By redefining success to focus on growth, effort, and influence, we can create a more meaningful and empowering way of living.

The Problem with Traditional Success Metrics

Traditional views of success are heavily outcome-driven. They emphasize tangible results, such as promotions, accolades, or wealth, while often ignoring the journey and personal growth required to achieve them. This focus on outcomes fosters a sense of control, as if reaching these milestones is solely dependent on our efforts.

However, life is rarely that predictable. External factors like market trends, timing, or sheer luck play significant roles in shaping outcomes. When we tie our self-worth to results, we set ourselves up for frustration and disappointment when things don't go as planned. Worse, the pressure to achieve can lead to burnout, perfectionism, and a constant sense of "never enough."

Shifting the Focus to Growth

A growth-oriented mindset redefines success as the process of learning, improving, and adapting rather than achieving specific outcomes. This perspective celebrates effort, persistence, and resilience, regardless of the end result.

For example, consider an artist who creates a painting. Traditional success might judge the painting's worth based on how much it sells for or how many people admire it. A growth-focused view, however, values the creative process—the skills learned, the joy of expression, and the courage to share something personal with the world.

By focusing on growth, we shift from external validation to internal fulfillment. Success becomes about how much we've learned, how far we've come, and how we've influenced the world around us.

The Role of Effort in Redefining Success

Effort is a key component of meaningful success. Unlike outcomes, which are often beyond our control, effort is something we can influence. Putting in consistent effort allows us to develop skills, build confidence, and create opportunities.

For instance, a student aiming to improve their grades might not achieve straight A's immediately. However, their dedication to studying, seeking help, and applying feedback demonstrates effort and growth. Over time, these efforts compound, leading to greater understanding and confidence.

Recognizing effort as a form of success helps us appreciate the journey and stay motivated, even when progress feels slow. It also encourages a sense of gratitude for the lessons and experiences we gain along the way.

Embracing Failure as Part of the Journey

Failure is often seen as the opposite of success, but it's actually a vital part of the process. Every setback provides valuable feedback and an opportunity to grow. When we embrace failure as a stepping stone rather than a dead end, we build resilience and creativity.

Consider an entrepreneur launching a new business. They might face initial struggles, such as limited customers or financial challenges. Instead of viewing these obstacles as failures, they can use them as opportunities to refine their approach, learn about their market, and develop innovative solutions. Each attempt brings them closer to their goal while teaching lessons that wouldn't be learned through success alone.

Aligning Success with Personal Values

True success is deeply personal. It aligns with who your true self is and your sense of purpose. When you define success on your own terms, it becomes a source of fulfillment rather than pressure.

For example, someone who values community might measure success by the relationships they build and the impact they have on others. A person who values creativity might define success by the joy they find in self-expression. Aligning your actions with your values ensures that your pursuit of success feels authentic and rewarding.

Practical Steps to Redefine Success

1. **Reflect on Your Values:** Identify what matters most to you and use these values to guide your definition of success.

2. **Set Growth-Oriented Goals:** Focus on goals that prioritize learning, effort, and personal development over specific outcomes.

3. **Celebrate Small Wins:** Acknowledge and applaud the progress you make along the way, no matter how small the success is.

4. **Embrace Feedback:** Use setbacks and constructive criticism as opportunities to grow and improve.

5. **Focus on Influence:** Recognize the ways your actions and presence positively impact others, even if the results aren't immediate.

The Freedom of Redefining Success

Letting go of traditional success metrics frees us from the burden of comparison and perfectionism. It allows us to pursue our passions, honor our values, and find joy in the journey. By focusing on growth, effort, and influence, we create a more fulfilling and sustainable path to success.

Review Questions

1. How have traditional success metrics influenced your sense of self-worth?

2. Reflect on a recent experience where you prioritized effort over outcome. How did it impact your perspective?

3. What values are most important to you, and how can they guide your definition of success?

4. How can embracing failure as part of the process help you achieve long-term growth and fulfillment?

CHAPTER 12

EMBRACING INFLUENCE AND LETTING GO

"Imagine waking up every day free from the weight of others' expectations, unburdened by the need to control every outcome. What if living authentically—aligning with your values and embracing your true self—was the key to that freedom? In a world that tempts us to conform, authenticity isn't just a choice; it's an act of courage."

Authenticity is the structural base of a meaningful and fulfilling life. Living authentically means keeping your actions aligned with your values, expressing your true self, and embracing your unique journey. Yet, the illusion of control often pulls us away from authenticity. It tempts us to conform to societal expectations, seek external validation, and focus on outcomes rather than the process of living. By letting go of control and focusing on influence, we can reclaim our authenticity and live with greater freedom and purpose.

What Does It Mean to Live Authentically?

Living authentically means being true to yourself. It's about understanding your values, passions, and beliefs and letting them guide your decisions and actions. Authenticity requires self-awareness, courage, and a willingness to embrace vulnerability.

For example, someone who values creativity might prioritize time for artistic expression, even if it doesn't lead to financial gain or external recognition. Their personal fulfillment comes from staying true to their passion rather than conforming to societal standards of success.

The Barriers to Authentic Living

While authenticity is deeply rewarding, it's not always easy to achieve. Several factors can hinder our ability to live authentically:

1. **Social Pressure:** Society often promotes rigid definitions of success and normalcy. These pressures can make us feel obligated to follow a certain path, even if it doesn't align with our true selves.

2. **Fear of Judgment:** This mental fear of being judged can lead us to hide our true selves and conform to others' expectations.

3. **The Illusion of Control:** Believing we must manage every aspect of our lives can pull us away from authenticity. Instead of focusing on what truly matters, we may chase perfection or external approval.

Letting Go of Control to Embrace Authenticity

Letting go of control is a key step in living authentically. It allows us to focus on what we can influence and accept what lies beyond our reach. This shift frees us from the pressure to conform or meet unrealistic expectations, enabling us to align our actions with our values.

For instance, a professional who values family might choose to prioritize work-life balance over climbing the corporate ladder.

By letting go of the need to meet societal expectations, they can focus on what truly matters to them.

The Role of Influence in Authentic Living

Influence empowers us to live authentically by focusing on what we can contribute rather than what we can control. When we act with intention and align our actions with our values, we naturally influence the world around us in positive ways.

Consider a community leader who advocates for environmental sustainability. They can't control how everyone else behaves, but they can influence others through education, advocacy, and leading by example. By staying true to their values, they inspire others to take action.

The Freedom of Vulnerability

Authenticity requires vulnerability—the will power and ability to show up as your true self, even when it feels scary and uncomfortable. Vulnerability is not a weakness; it's a strength that fosters connection and trust. When we allow ourselves to be seen, we create deeper, more meaningful relationships.

For example, sharing a personal struggle with a friend can deepen the bond and create a sense of mutual support. Vulnerability invites others to do the same, fostering authenticity in both parties.

Practical Steps to Live Authentically

1. **Identify Your Core Values:** Reflect on what matters most to you and use these values as a guide for your decisions and actions.

2. **Practice Self-Awareness:** Regularly check in with yourself to ensure your actions align with your values and passions.

3. **Set Boundaries:** Protect your time, energy, and well-being by saying no to commitments or expectations that don't align with your authentic self.

4. **Embrace Imperfection:** Let go of the need to be perfect and accept yourself as you are. Authenticity is about being real, not flawless.

5. **Seek people you can truly connect with:** Surround yourself with people who support and encourage your authenticity. These relationships will help you stay true to yourself.

The Benefits of Authentic Living

Living authentically brings a sense of freedom, fulfillment, and peace. When you let go of the need to control or conform, you open yourself to new possibilities and deeper connections. Authenticity also enhances your influence, as people are naturally drawn to those who act with integrity and purpose.

Review Questions

1. Reflect on a time when you felt truly authentic. What made that experience meaningful?

2. What social pressures or fears of judgment have influenced your decisions in the past? How can you overcome them?

3. How can letting go of control help you align your actions with your core values?

4. What steps can you take to embrace vulnerability and deepen your connections with others?

CHAPTER 13

THE EMPOWERMENT OF INFLUENCE

"Control is an illusion, but influence is a force—fluid, empowering, and capable of sparking real change. What if the key to shaping your world lies not in managing outcomes, but in aligning your actions with intention and letting your influence ripple outward?"

Influence is one of the greatest powers we possess. Unlike control, which is restrictive and often ineffective, influence is fluid, adaptable, and empowering. When we understand and embrace our ability to influence, we unlock the potential to create meaningful change in our lives and the world around us. This chapter explores how embracing influence empowers us to act with intention, navigate challenges, and inspire others.

Influence vs. Control

The key difference between influence and control lies in their approach to power. Control seeks to impose outcomes through direct force or strict management. Influence, on the other hand, works by inspiring, guiding, and shaping possibilities. It acknowledges the interconnected nature of life and leverages our actions, words, and presence to create impact.

For example, a manager who micromanages their team might achieve short-term compliance but stifles creativity and motivation. In contrast, a manager who empowers their team through trust and collaboration fosters innovation and engagement. By focusing on influence, they create an environment where people feel valued and motivated to contribute their best.

The Empowering Nature of Influence

Influence is empowering because it focuses on what we can do rather than what we cannot. It shifts our attention from external outcomes to internal actions, fostering a sense of purpose and agency. When we embrace influence, we stop chasing unattainable control and start leveraging our unique strengths to make a difference.

For instance, consider someone advocating for a cause they're passionate about, such as environmental conservation. While they cannot control how others will respond, they can influence awareness and behavior by sharing information, organizing events, and leading by example. Each action, no matter how small, contributes to the broader movement and creates ripples of change.

Cultivating Influence Through Intention

Intentionality is the foundation of effective influence. Acting with intention means aligning your actions with your values, goals, and desired impact. It requires clarity about what you stand for and how you want to contribute.

To cultivate influence through intention:

1. **Clarify Your Values:** Identify the principles that guide your decisions and actions.

2. **Set Meaningful Goals:** Focus on goals that align with your values and allow you to make a positive impact.

3. **Act with Purpose:** Approach each action with thoughtfulness and alignment to your greater purpose.

4. **Reflect and Adjust:** Regularly assess your actions and their outcomes to ensure they align with your intentions.

The Ripple Effect of Influence

One of the most powerful aspects of influence is its ripple effect. When we act with integrity and purpose, our influence extends far beyond the immediate situation. It inspires others to reflect, act, and create positive change in their own lives.

For example, a teacher who demonstrates kindness and curiosity not only influences their students but also shapes how those students interact with others. These students carry the lessons they've learned into their families, communities, and future endeavors, amplifying the teacher's influence.

Overcoming Barriers to Influence

While influence is empowering, it's not without its challenges. Common barriers include:

1. **Self-Doubt:** Believing that your actions don't matter can limit your willingness to act. Remember, influence often works in subtle and unexpected ways.

2. **Fear of Rejection:** Worrying about how others will respond can prevent you from sharing your ideas or taking initiative. Focus on your intentions rather than external reactions.

3. **Lack of Clarity:** Unclear values or goals can dilute your influence. Take time to reflect on what truly matters to you and how you want to contribute.

Practical Steps to Strengthen Your Influence

1. **Start Small:** Focus on actions within your immediate sphere of influence. Small changes often lead to larger impacts over time.

2. **Lead by Example:** Model the behavior and values you wish to see in others. Authenticity and consistency build trust and inspire change.

3. **Communicate Effectively:** Use clear, compassionate, and persuasive communication to share your ideas and inspire others.

4. **Build Relationships:** Influence is rooted in connection. Invest time in building meaningful relationships based on trust and mutual respect.

5. **Stay Resilient:** Influence takes time. Stay committed to your values and trust the process, even when progress feels slow.

The Joy of Empowering Others

One of the most rewarding aspects of influence is the opportunity to empower others. When we support others, we create a ripple effect of positivity and possibility. Empowering others involves:

- Encouraging their strengths and talents.

- Supporting their goals and aspirations.

- Celebrating their successes without comparison.

For example, a mentor who takes the time to guide and encourage their mentee not only helps that individual grow but also contributes to a culture of support and collaboration.

Embracing the Freedom of Influence

When we embrace influence, we free ourselves from the frustration and rigidity of control. Influence allows us to act with purpose, connect authentically, and create meaningful change without the pressure of managing every detail. It empowers us to live with intention and leave a positive legacy.

Review Questions

1. Reflect on a time when your actions created a ripple effect. How did it make you feel?

2. What values guide your actions, and how can you align them more closely with your influence?

3. How can overcoming self-doubt or fear of rejection strengthen your ability to influence others?

4. What steps can you take to empower those around you and amplify your impact?

CHAPTER 14

THE ONGOING JOURNEY OF UNIVERSE KNOWLEDGE

"What if the key to peace isn't holding on tighter, but learning to let go? Letting go isn't giving up—it's freeing yourself from what you can't control and discovering the power of acceptance. This chapter invites you to step into that freedom and embrace life's endless possibilities."

L etting go is one of the most amazing acts of being liberated we can undertake in life. When we release the illusion of control, we free ourselves from unnecessary stress, frustration, and fear. Letting go is not about giving up; it's about accepting reality, embracing change, and focusing on what truly matters. This chapter explores the freedom and empowerment that come from letting go and how it opens the door to greater peace and authenticity.

What Does Letting Go Really Mean?

Letting go means releasing attachment to outcomes, expectations, or situations that are beyond our influence. It involves acknowledging the limits of our control and choosing to focus on what we can influence instead. Letting go is an act of courage and trust—a decision to accept uncertainty and move forward with grace.

For example, consider someone who has been holding onto anger over a past conflict. By letting go of the need to change what has already happened, they free themselves from the emotional burden and open space for healing and growth.

Why Is Letting Go So Difficult?

Letting go can be scary and tough because it requires us to confront uncertainty and vulnerability. It's natural to want to hold onto control as a way of feeling safe and secure. However, this attachment often leads to more stress and disappointment, especially when things don't go as planned.

Fear of the unknown is another obstacle. Letting go means stepping into uncharted territory, which can feel uncomfortable or risky. But by embracing this discomfort, we pave the way for new opportunities and experiences.

The Emotional Benefits of Letting Go

When we let go, we experience a profound sense of relief and freedom. The emotional benefits include:

1. **Reduced Stress:** Letting go of the need to control everything allows us to relax and focus on what truly matters.

2. **Greater Clarity:** Acceptance clears mental clutter, helping us see situations more clearly and make better decisions.

3. **Improved Relationships:** Releasing expectations of others fosters healthier, more authentic connections.

4. **Increased Resilience:** Letting go helps us adapt to change and bounce back from setbacks.

Letting Go of Perfectionism

Perfectionism is one of the most common forms of attachment. The belief that we must achieve perfection in every area of life creates unnecessary pressure and prevents us from appreciating our efforts. Letting go of perfectionism means embracing imperfection as part of the human experience.

For example, a writer might delay finishing a project because it doesn't feel "perfect." By letting go of this expectation, they can complete their work and share it with others, focusing on progress rather than flawlessness.

Practical Steps to Let Go

1. **Acknowledge Your Attachments:** Reflect on areas where you feel stuck or overly invested. Ask yourself, "Am I trying to control something beyond my influence?"

2. **Practice Acceptance:** Accept reality as it is, rather than how you wish it to be. This doesn't mean giving up; it means working with what you have.

3. **Shift Your Focus:** Redirect your energy toward what you can influence, such as your actions, attitudes, and choices.

4. **Embrace Change:** See change as a real opportunity for growing rather than a threat. Each new experience brings valuable lessons.

5. Practice Gratitude: Focus on the positive aspects of your life. Gratitude helps shift your perspective from lack to abundance.

The Role of Influence in Letting Go

Letting go doesn't mean passivity. It's about channeling your energy into areas where you can make a difference. By focusing on influence, you create positive change without becoming attached to specific outcomes.

For example, a teacher might let go of the need to ensure every student excels but instead focus on creating an engaging and supportive learning environment. This approach empowers students while relieving the teacher of undue stress.

Stories of Letting Go

Real-life stories of letting go can inspire us to embrace this practice. For instance, consider a business owner who faced a sudden market downturn. Instead of trying to control external factors, they adapted their business model and found new opportunities. By letting go of their initial plans, they discovered resilience and innovation.

Another example is a parent who lets go of expecting their child to follow a specific path. They foster a stronger, more authentic relationship by supporting their child's unique journey.

The Freedom That Follows

The freedom of letting go is transformative. It allows us to:

- Live more authentically, without the weight of unrealistic expectations.
- Use your focus to be present in this moment rather than worrying about the past or future.
- Cultivate deeper connections with ourselves and others.
- Approach life with curiosity, openness, and joy.

Letting go is not a one-time act; it's an ongoing practice. Each time we release an attachment, we make room for growth, possibility, and peace.

Review Questions

1. Reflect on an area of your life where you've been holding onto control. What would letting go look like in this situation?

2. How has perfectionism affected your ability to take action or enjoy your accomplishments?

3. What steps can you take to practice acceptance and focus on what you can influence?

4. How can letting go foster greater freedom and authenticity in your relationships?

CHAPTER 15

CULTIVATING RESILIENCE THROUGH INFLUENCE

"Life's toughest moments test more than your strength—they reveal your resilience. It's not about avoiding hardships but rising to meet them, learning to influence your response, and emerging stronger. Ready to uncover the power that transforms obstacles into opportunities?"

Life is full of challenges and uncertainties, but resilience allows us to navigate them with strength and adaptability. Resilience is not about avoiding difficulties; it's about how we respond and recover when they arise. By focusing on influence instead of control, we can cultivate resilience and face life's ups and downs with confidence and purpose. This chapter explores how influence helps build resilience and provides practical strategies for fostering this essential skill.

What is Resilience?

Resilience is the superpower to bounce back from adversity and adapt to change. It's not a genetic trait but an increasing skill that can be developed over time. Resilient people are not immune to stress or hardship, but they have the tools to cope effectively and emerge stronger from their experiences.

For example, consider someone who loses their job unexpectedly. A resilient response might involve processing the emotions, seeking support, and taking proactive steps to find new opportunities. While the situation is challenging, resilience helps them move forward rather than staying stuck in frustration or despair.

The Role of Influence in Resilience

Influence plays a crucial role in resilience because it shifts our focus from what we can't control to what we can affect. When faced with adversity, it's easy to feel powerless. However, by identifying areas of influence, we regain a sense of agency and empowerment.

For instance, during a natural disaster, individuals cannot control the weather or the extent of the damage. Still, they can influence their response by helping neighbors, securing resources, or staying informed. These actions not only contribute to recovery but also foster a sense of purpose and connection.

Building Resilience Through Mindset

Resilience begins with a mindset that embraces growth, adaptability, and optimism. This mindset allows us to see challenges as opportunities for learning and growth rather than insurmountable obstacles.

1. **Commit to a Growth Mindset:** View what you thought was failure as opportunity to learn and improve. Instead of thinking, "I failed," reframe it as, "What can I learn from this experience?"

2. **Practice Optimism:** Focus on what is possible rather than dwelling on what went wrong. Optimism doesn't mean ignoring difficulties but approaching them with hope and determination.

3. **Embrace Change:** Accept that change is a natural part of life and an opportunity for growth. Resilient people adapt to new circumstances rather than resisting them.

Developing Emotional Resilience

Emotional resilience is the ability to identify stress and maintain your emotional balance during tough or adverse times. It involves understanding and regulating our emotions while staying connected to our inner strength.

1. **Practice Self-Awareness:** Recognize your emotions and what triggers them. Understanding your feelings helps you respond intentionally rather than react impulsively.

2. **Cultivate Self-Compassion:** Be kind to yourself during difficult times. Show yourself the same compassion and understanding you would offer your dear friend.

3. **Fortify yourself with Emotional Support:** Surround yourself with people who uplift and encourage you. Sharing your struggles with trusted friends or family can ease emotional burdens.

Strengthening Resilience Through Connection

Resilience is often strengthened through connection with others. Relationships provide support, encouragement, and perspective, helping us navigate challenges more effectively.

1. **Foster Community:** Engage with groups or communities that share your values and goals. These connections provide a sense of belonging and mutual support.

2. **Help Others:** Supporting others in their struggles can reinforce your own resilience. Acts of kindness and service create a sense of purpose and remind us of our ability to make a difference.

3. **Discover mentors:** Learning from others who have overcome similar challenges can provide valuable insights and inspiration.

Practical Strategies for Building Resilience

1. **Focus on Small Wins:** Celebrate small achievements to build momentum and confidence. Each step forward reinforces your ability to overcome challenges.

2. **Set Realistic Goals:** Break larger challenges into manageable steps. This approach reduces overwhelm and keeps you moving forward.

3. **Make Self-Care Mandatory:** Increase activities that nurture and help heal your physical, emotional, and mental well-being. Exercise, sleep, and mindfulness practices are essential for maintaining resilience.

4. **Live a Life More Flexible:** Be willing to adjust your plans and expectations as circumstances change. Flexibility helps you adapt and find new solutions.

Stories of Resilience

Real-life examples of resilience can inspire and motivate us to cultivate our own. For instance, consider an athlete recovering from a serious injury. Instead of giving up, they focus on rehabilitation, set small goals, and eventually return stronger than before. Their journey demonstrates the power of determination, adaptability, and influence.

Another example is a single parent balancing work and family responsibilities. Despite the challenges, they draw strength from their love for their children and their commitment to creating a better future. Their resilience shines through in their ability to adapt and persevere.

The Freedom of Resilience

Resilience offers a profound sense of freedom. It empowers us to face challenges without being overwhelmed, to adapt to change without losing our sense of self, and to grow stronger through adversity. By focusing on influence, we can navigate life's uncertainties with confidence and purpose.

Review Questions

1. Reflect on a time when you faced adversity. How did your mindset and actions influence your ability to overcome it?

2. What steps can you take to build emotional resilience and maintain balance during difficult times?

3. How can fostering connections with others strengthen your resilience?

4. What small actions can you take today to cultivate a more resilient mindset?

CHAPTER 16

THE RIPPLE EFFECT OF LETTING GO

"Every action we take sends ripples into the world—some small, some monumental, but all significant. What kind of waves are you creating?"

The way we live, the choices we make, and the influence we exert don't stop with us. They ripple outward, touching the lives of those around us and often extending further than we realize. By letting go of control and embracing influence, we not only transform our own lives but also create waves of positive change in the world. This chapter explores the ripple effect of letting go and how our actions inspire and influence others.

The Nature of the Ripple Effect

Every action we take sends ripples into the world. These ripples may be as simple as a smile that brightens someone's day or as profound as a movement that changes lives. The ripple effect reminds us that our influence is powerful, even when it seems small or indirect.

For example, consider a teacher who inspires students to think critically and pursue their passions. Those students carry the lessons they've learned into their lives, influencing their families, friends, and communities. The teacher's influence extends far beyond the classroom, creating a legacy of growth and inspiration.

Letting Go to Create Space for Influence

Letting go of control allows us to focus on what truly matters and act with authenticity. When we stop trying to manage every detail, we create space for genuine connection and meaningful action. This openness invites others to engage with us in a more authentic way, amplifying our influence.

For instance, a manager who lets go of micromanaging their team allows employees to take ownership of their work. This trust fosters creativity, collaboration, and innovation, creating a positive ripple effect throughout the organization.

Inspiring Others Through Authenticity

Your authenticity is one of the most powerful ways you have available to influence others. When we live in alignment with our values and express our true selves, we inspire others to do the same. Authenticity builds trust and connection, making our influence more impactful.

Consider someone who openly shares their journey of overcoming challenges. Their vulnerability and honesty encourage others to reflect on their own experiences and find strength in their struggles. By being authentic, they create a ripple effect of empowerment and resilience.

The Role of Kindness in the Ripple Effect

Acts of kindness, even if they are small, have a profound impact. A kind word, a helping hand, or a moment of compassion can create ripples that extend far beyond the initial interaction. Kindness helps inspire others to pay it forward, making a chain reaction of positivity.

For example, a stranger who pays for someone's coffee might inspire that person to perform their own act of kindness, such as helping a neighbor or volunteering. These small gestures build a sense of community and connection, reinforcing the idea that our actions matter.

Overcoming Barriers to Influence

While the ripple effect is powerful, it can be hindered by self-doubt, fear of judgment, or a belief that our actions don't make a difference. Overcoming these barriers involves:

1. **Recognizing Your Impact:** Acknowledge that your actions, no matter how small, contribute to the world around you.

2. **Acting with Intention:** Focus on actions that align with your values and create positive change.

3. **Trusting the Process:** Understand that influence often works subtly and over time. Trust that your efforts will have an impact, even if you don't see immediate results.

Building a Legacy of Influence

A legacy is not about wealth, fame, or achievements. It's about the positive impact we leave behind and the lives we touch. By living with intention and embracing influence, we create a legacy that inspires others to carry forward our values and actions.

For example, a parent who prioritizes empathy and kindness models these values for their children. Those children, in turn, bring these qualities into their own relationships, creating a generational ripple effect of compassion and understanding.

Practical Ways to Amplify Your Ripple Effect

1. **Be the Example:** Be the behaviors and values you want to see in others. Authenticity and consistency build trust and inspire change.

2. **Cultivate Connection:** Invest in meaningful relationships and create spaces for open dialogue and collaboration.

3. **Practice Gratitude:** Express appreciation for others' efforts and contributions. Gratitude strengthens relationships and encourages positive actions.

4. **Encourage Others:** Support and uplift those around you. Celebrate their successes and help them recognize their own influence.

The Freedom of Letting Go

Letting go of control and embracing influence allows us to live with greater freedom and purpose. It frees us from the pressure to manage everything and invites us to focus on what truly matters. This freedom not only enhances our own lives but also amplifies our ability to create positive change.

Review Questions

1. Reflect on a time when your actions created a positive ripple effect. How did it make you feel?

2. How can letting go of control create space for greater influence in your life?

3. What small actions can you take today to inspire and uplift those around you?

4. How can you build a legacy of influence that aligns with your values?

CHAPTER 17

THE EMPOWERED LIFE

"What if everything you thought you controlled was an illusion? Real power isn't found in managing life's chaos but in the quiet strength of your influence. This is where freedom begins."

The journey through this book has been about rediscovering your power, not the power to control, but the power to influence. By letting go of control, embracing influence, and living authentically, you open yourself to a life of freedom, connection, and purpose. This chapter ties together the themes we've explored and serves as a call to action for living an empowered life.

Reflecting on the Illusion of Control

Throughout this journey, we've dismantled the myth of control. From the smallest daily routines to the grandest life plans, control is an illusion we cling to for comfort. Yet, this illusion often leads to frustration, anxiety, and disconnection.

We've seen how this need for control infiltrates our relationships, careers, and personal aspirations. It's natural to want stability and predictability, but life's dynamic and ever-changing nature makes absolute control impossible. The more we try to control every detail, the more friction we create, and the more likely we are to feel trapped by our own efforts.

By letting go of control, we free ourselves from the impossible task of managing the uncontrollable. We learn to navigate life with grace, focusing on what we can influence and finding peace in the process. Letting go allows us to accept life as it is, rather than how we wish it to be. This acceptance is not resignation but a shift in perspective that opens the door to freedom and empowerment.

Embracing Influence as True Power

Influence is subtle yet profound. It's the ability to shape outcomes, inspire change, and create ripples of positivity through your actions and presence. Unlike control, influence respects the dynamic and interconnected nature of life. It empowers you to act with intention, align with your values, and impact the world in meaningful ways.

Consider how influence has played a role in your life. Reflect on the moments when your words, actions, or choices made a difference, even in small ways. Perhaps you encouraged a friend during a difficult time, and their gratitude inspired you to be more supportive in other relationships. Or maybe you shared your passion for a cause, sparking interest and action in those around you. These moments remind us that true power lies not in control but in our ability to inspire and uplift.

Influence also invites collaboration. When we focus on influence, we recognize that our efforts are part of a larger web of actions and connections. This perspective fosters humility and strengthens our relationships, as we see ourselves not as isolated agents but as contributors to a shared experience.

Living Authentically and Resiliently

Living authentically means aligning your actions with your values, embracing vulnerability, and letting go of societal expectations. Resilience, on the other hand, gives you the strength to adapt, grow, and thrive in the face of challenges.

Together, authenticity and resilience form the foundation of an empowered life.

Authenticity requires self-awareness and courage. It means being honest with yourself about what matters most and making choices that reflect your true self. This authenticity might involve saying no to opportunities that don't align with your values or taking risks to pursue a passion. While authenticity can feel vulnerable, it also fosters deeper connections and greater fulfillment.

Resilience complements authenticity by helping you navigate setbacks and uncertainties with grace. When you face challenges, resilience enables you to learn, adapt, and move forward. It's not about avoiding difficulties but about growing stronger through them. By combining resilience with authenticity, you create a life that feels true to who you are and adaptable to whatever comes your way.

The Freedom of Letting Go

Letting go is not about giving up; it's about accepting what is and focusing on what matters most. This freedom allows you to live with less stress, more joy, and a deeper sense of purpose. It invites you to stop chasing outcomes and start appreciating the journey.

Imagine waking up each day with a sense of possibility rather than pressure, knowing that you don't need to control everything to make a difference. This possibility thinking is the freedom that comes from embracing influence and letting go of control. It's the freedom to focus on the present moment, to act with intention, and to trust the process.

Letting go also enhances your relationships. When you release the need to control others, you create space for mutual respect, understanding, and collaboration. This shift fosters deeper connections and allows your influence to flourish naturally.

A Call to Action: Living the Empowered Life

Living an empowered life is not a destination; it's a practice. It's about choosing daily to act with intention, focus on influence, and let go of what you cannot control. It's about finding joy in the journey and creating a legacy of positivity and growth.

As you move forward, consider these guiding principles:

1. **Align Your Actions with Your Values:** Reflect on what matters most to you and let your values guide your decisions.

2. **Embrace Vulnerability:** Allow yourself to be seen and express your true self, even when it feels uncomfortable.

3. **Focus on Influence:** Identify areas where your actions can make a difference and act with intention.

4. **Practice Resilience:** Approach challenges as opportunities for growth, and trust in your ability to adapt and thrive.

5. **Celebrate the Journey:** Acknowledge your progress, appreciate the lessons, and find joy in the process of living authentically.

Reflecting on Your Journey

The lessons in this book are not just concepts to understand but practices to integrate into your daily life. As you reflect on what you've learned, think about how these principles have already begun to shape your perspective and actions. Consider how letting go of control, embracing influence, and living authentically can enhance your relationships, goals, and overall well-being.

Remember, this journey you are on is not about perfection but about progress. Each step you take toward living an empowered life is a step toward greater freedom, connection, and purpose.

Review Questions

1. Reflect on your journey through this book. What insights have resonated with you the most, and how can you apply them in your daily life?

2. How has your understanding of control and influence changed, and what impact has this shift had on your mindset?

3. What steps will you take to live authentically and align your actions with your values moving forward?

4. How can embracing influence and letting go of control enhance your relationships, goals, and overall well-being?

ABOUT THE AUTHOR

Mike Jensen II is a Life Performance Coach with over 12 years of experience helping individuals achieve the greatest performance of their lives and live up to their potential. He holds several certifications in Energy Leadership, Mental Toughness Training, Professional Coaching, and the Science of Happiness. Mike writes a daily short blog on various social media platforms under MBR3 Coaching, which has been updated every day for over eight years without fail. His blog focuses on encouraging others to think outside the box, recognize the abundance around them, and choose a different way to live.

When he's not writing or blogging, Mike is coaching clients all over the world. In his personal time, he enjoys spending time with his amazing wife, family, and especially his grandchildren. Although Mike has lived all over the United States, he always returns to Ottawa, Kansas, a small town he loves for its smallness, slowness, and quietness.

Mike has dedicated his life to serving others, helping them find sustainable happiness and live up to their potential. He believes that everyone has a purpose and unlimited potential.

ABOUT THE PUBLISHER

Dear Reader,

As you hold this remarkable book in your hands, we want to express our heartfelt gratitude for becoming a part of the Live Life Happy Community of readers. Your curiosity and thirst for knowledge fuel our passion for publishing meaningful non-fiction works.

At Live Life Happy Publishing, our mission is rooted in bringing forth literature that not only entertains but uplifts, supports, and nourishes the soul. We firmly believe that books have the power to transform lives, to ignite passions, and to spread joy far and wide.

Behind every word, every chapter, lies the dedication of our authors who pour their hearts and souls into their craft. Their ultimate aim? To touch your life in profound ways, to inspire, and to leave an indelible mark on your journey.

Your role in this journey is invaluable; by sharing your thoughts through reviews, spreading the word to others, or reaching out to the authors themselves, you become an integral part of sparking transformation in countless lives, igniting a ripple effect of joy and enlightenment.

And if, perchance, you or someone you know has dreams of writing, of sharing a message, or of unleashing a powerful story unto the world, know that Live Life Happy Publishing stands ready to guide you. Our doors are open, our ears attuned, and our hearts eager to hear your message.

So, dear reader, let us, continue to spread the power of literature, one page at a time. Reach out, share, and most importantly, never underestimate the power of your message to touch lives.

With warmest regards,

LiveLifeHappyPublishing.com

P.S. Remember, books change lives. Whose life will you touch with yours?